A YEAR OF
EDUCATIONAL
QUIET BINS

The secret to peaceful days at home
with kids.

Sarah Noftle, BA, B. Ed.

A Year of Educational Quiet Bins

The secret to peaceful days at home with kids.

Photography by Sarah Noftle.

CONTENTS

4

Once Upon a Time...

Once upon a time, in a land near yet far, there lived a Mama. This Mama wanted nothing more than to stay home with her kids. She longed for those long, sunny days full of finger painting, stories, and snuggles. Those moments of connection, watching all those incredible firsts, and hearing those tiny voices all day long.

Well, one day, that wish came true. Mama was able to stay home with her kids all day long. All. Day. Long. She enjoyed many long, sunny days full of finger painting, stories, and snuggles. She also watched all those amazing firsts and heard those tiny voices all day long. All. Day. Long. At first, it was absolutely blissful. But then...

Then the stormy clouds of childhood rolled in. Those days that every Mama has, but few have the energy to speak of. Those days when the pink sippy cup repulses a child and reduces him to a weeping, melty toddler pile on the floor. Those days when you have been bitten, screeched at, and the children seem to be magnetized (loud, disagreeable magnets). Those days that make any Mama wonder, what had gone so wrong?

So then, as all Mamas do, this Mama picked herself up (and picked a few books up too). She learned some new things, some new skills, and some new information. She armed herself with a new way of being home with her children. A way, she hoped, that would restore peace to her kingdom once more. (Because at this point in our story, this Mama becomes a Queen).

Queen Mama proclaimed to her royal family that there would be no more hardships, no more biting, no more child screeching. Instead, we would be implementing a simple, beautiful rhythm to our day. A rhythm that respects childhood, and embraces the needs of children. A rhythm which allows our daily needs and activities to occur, but in a manner that does not overwhelm; allowing everyone in the kingdom to get what they really need in order to live happily ever after.

Much to the surprise of Queen Mama – it worked! It worked so very well that this Mama decided she must write a royal proclamation telling all of the Queen Mamas (and Teachers and Daddies and Caregivers and anyone who even makes eye contact with children) about this beautiful rhythm and the magic that is QUIET BINS.

The End.

(But of course it is not the end. "The Start" just didn't look right.)

IMPLEMENTING A RHYTHM

The rhythm that I have implemented in my household is based loosely on Rudolph Steiners Waldorf pedagogy. I will not go into too much detail about his approach as there are hundreds, if not thousands, of books written solely on this topic already. I am far from an expert in that area, so I will leave that to those who are. However, I will recommend some books if you are interested in learning more about Steiner and Waldorf Education at the end of this book.

The basic principles I have taken into my household are twofold:

The first is that children need ample free time. Loads of time to play outside and in, uninterrupted.

The second, which is actually the reason for this book, is that children need to rotate between "expansions" and "contractions" in their days. Much like breathing, they need to swap between these two ways of being in order to be peaceful, happy, and learning.

An expansion can be thought of as a breath in and is very natural for children. Actively playing and running occur during an expansion. These boys of mine are excellent at 'expanding.' I used to believe that little ones needed to blow off steam and would stack busy activities on top of other busy activities expecting to tire my boys out. But this often resulted in meltdowns and tantrums. I was simply just missing the second part.

A contraction, in this sense, can be thought of as a breath out. Just as important as the breath in, it must in fact occur before another breath can effectively be taken. A contraction is a time of quiet. Art, stories, and quiet songs are all contraction activities.

Transitioning to contractions tend to be much harder on toddlers and preschoolers than transitioning to an expansion. Little ones generally find it more challenging to sit down and read a story after racing around like a jet plane.

This was precisely the issue that I was having with my boys. I could see the beauty of this rhythm and how it would work well for my children. I had even seen, when I had been successful in alternating them from a busy time to a quiet time, a peacefulness that I hadn't seen in a long time. But it was tough for my boys to settle. We were struggling with the transition between an expansion and a contraction.

Until we started using Quiet Bins.

I use Quiet Bins all the time in my household. I use them to help pull the boys from a busy activity just before things go very wrong, much like a "transitional activity." If I want the boys to settle down before their rest time, I just pull out a Quiet Bin. If we have been playing outside and the boys need a break, a Quiet Bin will save us time and again. The activities have just enough structure to keep them engaged in quiet play.

But I use our Quiet Bins far more often that that! We use them during the dinner time witching hour, long car rides, waiting at appointments, in restaurants, during tricky wake ups or nights when a little extra quiet time is needed before bed. Quiet Bins have worked wonders in our household. I hope that they will in yours too.

OUR RHYTHM

6:30 Wake up. Children play on their own or watch a show while we get ready for the day.

7:15 Family breakfast.

7:45 Dad leaves for work. I help the boys get ready for the day: dressed, teeth brushed, beds made.

(So far our morning has been a "contraction" or quiet)

8:15 Outside play. Each morning we head outside to wait for the bus with my oldest child. The boys easily move into this expansion, running around, playing with the chickens, bouncing on the trampoline, swinging on the climber, anything goes.

I try to give the boys lots of unstructured outside time in the morning, but by about 9:30 things are generally starting to deteriorate and I can feel the need for a contraction.

9:30 Indoor quiet play. Usually the boys split up now playing quietly on their own: train tracks, blocks, independent things. This is an important piece to our rhythm, time alone. This is when I drink my very important cup of coffee and enjoy watching my boys play. If there is any trouble settling into this quiet play, then I will grab a Quiet Bin.

10:15 Morning outing. Usually we have an outing planned in the morning. Outings are almost always expansions for children – lots of sounds, sights, and new faces. We have gymnastics, playgroups, library visits, grocery shopping, parks to explore, etc.

12:00 Home to a Quiet Bin at the kitchen table while I make lunch. I have learned that my little ones are sensitive to food and sleep. They need a lot of both. Right before lunch my boys have trouble playing kindly, so I prevent any chaos by structuring their quiet time with a Quiet Bin.

12:30 Lunch

1:00 Rest. My toddler has a nap and my 5 year old has independent quiet time. This independent quiet time took us a little while to master. I did not want him sitting in front of the TV for an hour or more, but he needed a rest – and so did I. By pulling out a Quiet Bin in the middle of the playroom, I found he would quietly begin to explore the bin. This would settle him into his rest time, and he would be calm and move on to other quiet play activities in the room independently after this. It is still not perfect, but really quite good. Rest time lasts for about an hour and a half.

2:30 Wake up and Snack

2:45 Outside Play. My little ones wake up raring to go, so right after rest time and snack, they are set for an expansion. Usually, we head outside again to play and wait for the school bus.

3:45 Time for some quiet and another snack. The bus arrives so we head inside for another (little) snack.

4:00 At this point the kids usually play well together inside for a little while before the witching hour hits. I try to keep this a contraction with quiet activities, but the boys generally start to get a little rowdy.

4:30 Dad is home and the kids ease into a full expansion.

5:00 Quiet Bin while dinner is getting ready.

5:30 Family Dinner.

6:15 One last expansion, but not too busy. Depending on the day it is usually a walk or play.

6:45 Bedtime routine is started (pyjamas, teeth, stories, songs)

7:15 Sleep for the boys.

WHAT ARE QUIET BINS?

Quiet Bins can be amazingly simple to create, can include things you already have on hand, and can cost next to nothing – but they hold an incredible power. With just a little thought and time, Quiet Bins can be created to give children an incredible gift. The gift of assisting them through the sometimes rocky transition between an expansion and a contraction. That time when children need to slow down and quiet down, but are having a bit of trouble in doing so. Or during a time when quiet play is needed, like in a waiting room, restaurant, or on a long car ride.

Quiet Bins contain an activity. A simple, gently structured, independent activity. They also provide children with a focus while their little bodies transition from a busy time, or an expansion, to a quiet time, or a contraction.

Quiet Bins can be changed quite regularly to keep the activities engaging and fun. Usually, we have five Quiet Bins in our house and change the activities every other week. If the kids are still really engaged with a favourite box, then I will leave it and exchange the other four.

I like to draw on themes and interests when creating Quiet Bins. Since we are often outside, I like to organize my bins by seasons. This helps us pull on the greater rhythm of the year, as well. I also create Quiet Bins based on the interests of my little ones and any skills we have been working on at home.

Since Quiet Bins are independent, sometimes the activities inside are not used as I had intended them to be used, but this doesn't matter one bit. While the bins are educational, their true purpose is singular: to help little ones settle. As long as they are doing that, the bins are working like a charm.

Since I am a teacher, I ensure that each Quiet Bin holds educational value as well. Fine motor development, critical thinking skills, patterning, sorting, imaginative and creative thinking, letter and number learning, colour recognition, and independence to name just a few.

Winter Quiet Bins

Where we live it gets cold. Really cold. Some days it is just too cold to be outside. No outside time with busy little boys? We make it work. We alternate lots of running and playing downstairs with these engaging Winter Quiet Bins.

Build a snowman, make a snowflake necklace, play in a winter wonderland, or wrap a Christmas gift. Lots of engaging, quiet activities to help settle little ones this holiday season.

Paper Chain Countdown

Materials:

- Paper strips
- Tape
- Markers

Target skills:

- Counting
- One to one correspondence
- Fine motor skills

With the holiday season comes a whole lot of excitement. Whatever you are celebrating this holiday season, a countdown chain is sure to be a hit.

By creating a simple paper chain little ones can practice counting, numbers, and one-to-one correspondence (adding one chain for each day of the countdown).

When the chain is done it can be hung up and one link can be ripped off each day until finally the holiday arrives!

Elastic Wrapping

Materials:

- Small elastics

- Empty wrapping paper rolls

Target skills:

- Strengthening hands for writing

- Counting

- Colour sorting

Wrapping gifts? Put those empty wrapping paper rolls to good use.

Using small hair elastics wrapped around the thumb and first two fingers, little ones can stretch the elastics onto the sturdy wrapping paper roll.

This activity is fantastic for strengthening little hands for future writing.

It is also a great chance for children to practice counting or sorting by colours. Add a number to a roll and children can add that number of elastics. Add a colour to the roll, and sort by colour.

Christmas Tree Decorations

Materials:

- Small cardboard shapes
- Supplies for decorating, pipe cleaners

Target skills:

- Creative thinking
- Independence

This Quiet Bin hangs around our house from the beginning of November until the end of December. It is so simple to create and it is always a HUGE hit!

Simply add small cardboard shapes (bulbs, Christmas trees) with holes poked into the top and some decorating supplies. We use markers, stickers, stamps, ribbon, etc.

After decorations have been created, little ones can pop a pipe cleaner through the top and hook it onto the Christmas tree.

Cotton Ball Snowmen

Materials:

- Cotton balls

- Clear plastic cups

Target skills:

- Imaginative play

- Problem solving

- Sensory experience

Do you want to build a snowman?

Add a few clear plastic cups to a bin full of cotton balls and little ones can build snowmen that will stay all year long.

Draw some faces with permanent marker. Add some buttons to other cups the same way.

When the cups are filled they can be stacked to create little snowmen perfect for imaginative play.

Try drawing different emotions on the cup faces to add a new element to the play.

Snowflake Jewelry

Materials:

- White straws

- Snowflakes

- Beads

- Yarn

Target skills:

- Fine motor skills

- Estimation

Cutting straws is a great way to introduce scissor skills and cutting to children. They are sturdy and small enough to get snipped with just one snip.

Children can cut up white straws to make 'snowflake beads'. These beads can be threaded onto yarn to make bracelets, necklaces, and crowns.

This is a great time for children to begin to play with estimation. How long does the bracelet need to be to wrap around my arm? What about as a crown? Add some little snowflakes and beads too!

Wrap a Present

Materials:

- Small boxes

- Tiny gifts

- Wrapping paper

- Bows

- Gift tags

- Pencil

Target skills:

- Fine motor skills

- Kindness

Little ones love the chance to give gifts. Add a few little tokens (like stickers or tiny farm animals) for children to put inside the boxes and wrap as gifts for family.

Wrapping boxes is tricky, but fantastic for coordination development. Help little ones succeed by pre-cutting the paper and tape. Pre-cut tape can also be bought.

Don't forget the gift tags and a pencil to add in some literacy!

Button bracelets (in a Quiet Bin in the 'Anytime' section) make lovely gifts as well.

Snow Plough Town

Materials:

- White pompoms and cotton balls

- Little snow ploughs and dump trucks

Target skills:

- Imaginative play

Create a winter wonderland in this Quiet Bin!

Add tiny white pompoms and cotton balls, little trucks and ploughs, even small houses and people.

Children can create elaborate little stories about the people needing to get into town, but the road being too full of snow.

Pretty soon the trucks will be working hard, people will be getting where they need to go, and little ones will be quietly engaged in play.

Adding Snow

Materials:

- Photos glued onto cardboard with holes punched

- Long white yarn or pipe cleaner for lacing

Target skills:

- Fine motor skills

- Weaving

Do you have some photos of your last beach vacation? Or maybe a picture of the summer barbeque? Glue them onto some cardboard and poke holes all around the background (a small hole punch works well).

Add these photos to the Quiet Bin with long strands of white yarn and little ones can lace snow all over these pictures.

Of course this would work with any picture, but silly things (like adding snow to a photo of a child in a pool) is sure to engage little ones.

Colour Doilies

Materials:

- Paper doilies or snowflakes

- Blue crayons of different shades

Target skills:

- Creativity

- Patterning

- Fine motor skills

The result of this Quiet Bin is always beautiful.

Children can colour paper doilies (or paper snowflakes) using different shades of blue.

Children can work on fine motor control by colouring around the holes, and work on fine details by colouring the small spaces in between holes.

Older children can experiment with shading and playing with the use of colours.

Spring Quiet Bins

Spring is the time when we are outside again. A lot. My busy little ones get to run and swing and climb and spend their days outside.

But with all this busyness, we need Quiet Bins to help pull the boys in a little. Hmmm ... or more than a little. These Quiet Bins are perfect for helping little ones settle after being busy outside.

Make animal paddocks, play in the rain, create gorgeous Easter eggs, or bake some cupcakes this Spring.

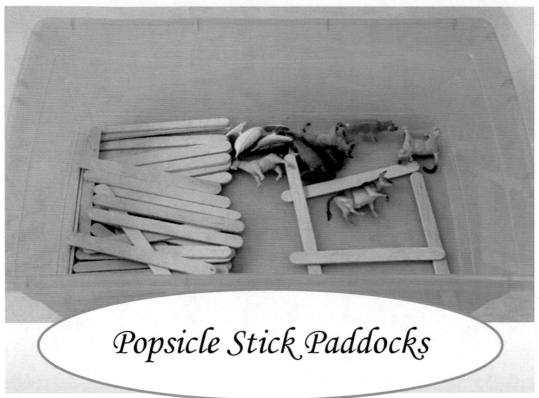

Popsicle Stick Paddocks

Materials:

- Popsicle sticks

- Farm animals

Target skills:

- Visual spatial skills

- Problem solving

Nice and simple, but full of possibilities. This Quiet Bin is one of my favourites.

Children can create paddocks for all of their farm animals: simple squares, rectangles, octagons, and so on. Older children can even build barns.

As they play, stories will unfold about the animals and problem solving will come into play. Perhaps the goat won't like to be next to the horse, or the chicken will escape! Only time will tell...Quiet time....

Rainbow Easter Eggs

Materials:

- Plastic or wooden Easter eggs

- Rainbow beads, buttons, or paper clips

Target skills:

- Colour matching

- Sorting

- Number recognition and counting

Spring is full of colour—and so is this Quiet Bin! Plastic Easter eggs and matching buttons and beads are very inviting for little ones.

This Quiet Bin can be used in many different ways. Sorting buttons and beads by colour or size into matching Easter eggs is a great activity.

Older children can look at numbers drawn on the eggs and put that number of beads and buttons inside to practice both number recognition and counting.

Colouring Easter Eggs

Materials:

- Printed Easter Eggs

- Markers or crayons

Target skills:

- Fine motor skills

- Increased concentration

A quick Google search for "Easter Egg Colouring Pages" will easily fill a Quiet Bin!

Print off many different Easter eggs (those with zigzag lines are fantastic for pre-writers) and cut them out. Pop them in a Quiet Bin with some markers or crayons.

Encourage little ones to colour the eggs completely. This activity is excellent for building focus and concentration.

Patterning and shading can also come into play for older children.

Felt Easter Egg Decorating

Materials:

- Felt Egg Shapes

- Felt lines, circles, etc.

Target skills:

- Fine motor skills

- Patterning

- Creativity

This Quiet Bin is a big hit with toddlers and can simply be customized to work on almost any area at all.

Cut out some egg shapes from felt using various colours. Use the left over scraps to cut out circles, lines, diamonds, and other shapes.

Little ones will have loads of quiet fun decorating their Easter eggs.

Sorting by shapes or colours, and counting skills can all easily be targeted with this Quiet Bin.

Make a Rainbow

Materials:

- Construction paper or foam paper arcs in various colours.

Target skills:

- Ordering
- Patterns

This Quiet Bin is easiest if constructed in this way:

Draw a rainbow on a piece of blank paper. Next, stack several different colours of construction paper behind that sheet. Finally cut out each arc of your rainbow, cutting through all of the paper at once.

You will be left with many arcs of different colours and sizes.

Children can make rainbows of solid colours, repeating patterns, or even learn about the Rainbow order (Red, Orange, Yellow, Green, Blue, Indigo, Violet)

Foam sheets make this activity amazingly durable.

Bake a Cupcake

Materials:

- Large Pompoms

- Cupcake liners

- Tiny felt pieces.

Target skills:

- Imaginative play

- Fine motor skills

Since Spring tends to be birthday season, I thought this Quiet Bin belonged in this section. Though, of course, it is a great bin to use during your child's birthday week.

Creating great big cupcakes is a great way to spark some imaginative play. Little ones will be having imaginary friends over to join them in their cupcake party in no time.

Adding little felt sprinkles to the cupcakes or tiny felt cherries on top is a great way to add some fine motor fun too.

Egg Carton Games

Materials:

- Egg Cartons

- Buttons, letters, stones, anything.

Target skills:

- This Quiet Bin can be used to practice anything at all.

Egg cartons provide little compartments perfect for sorting. Since Spring is the time for eggs (both Easter and on our farm when the ladies are finally laying again after the cold winter), I thought I would put this Quiet Bin in the Spring section. But it is great for anytime...or all the time!

Add capital letters to the compartments and have little ones sort lowercase magnet letters to match. Add numbers to the compartments and have children count that number of buttons into each spot. The options are endless!

Umbrella and Raindrops

Materials:

- Little drink umbrellas
- Tiny blue pompoms
- Little people

Target skills:

- Fine motor skills
- Imaginative play

April showers bring loads of quiet play...at least with this Quiet Bin!

Children love to play with tiny drink umbrellas—and better yet, the dexterity needed to open those little umbrellas is also strengthening those little hands for future writing.

Add some blue pompoms so little people can play in the rain and this Quiet Bin is sure to provide little ones with lots of room to stretch their imaginations.

Blossoming Branches

Materials:

- Brown and green pipe-cleaners

- Pink and purple beads and buttons

Target skills:

- Patterning

- Learning about nature lifecycles

- Fine motor skills

Spring is the time of blossoms coming back to the trees. This is such an amazing time of year, full of colour after the white of winter.

Little ones can play with creating their own blossoming branches with this Quiet Bin.

Children can thread on big purple buttons for flowers and smaller pink beads for blossoms.

These branches often turn into nature crowns and bracelets in our home.

Paper Cup Flowers

Materials:

- Small 'Dixie' cups cut along the sides

- Coloured paper clips

Target skills:

- Patterning

- Fine motor skills

- Counting

Create beautiful flowers while strengthening little hands this Spring.

To prepare this Quiet Bin, cut from the top of a small paper cup to the bottom all along the sides. Gently fold back the cup so it looks like petals.

Add lots of paper clips in beautiful colours for little ones to clip to each flower petal.

This activity is quite mesmerizing, as the flowers look very pretty as they are becoming full of paper clips.

Colours can be sorted and patterned as well.

Summer Quiet Bins

Soccer games? Baseball? A big family barbeque? With summer comes a lot of exciting events for little ones. These Quiet Bins are perfect for bringing along.

Many of these are great for a few children to do together, making them great for gatherings.

They are also easily transported and can be played with indoors or out.

Catch the popsicle drips, learn letters with watermelon seeds, or make a 'cheery' surprise for the birds this summer.

Watermelon Seed Tracing

Materials:

- Pink paper plates

- Black buttons

Target skills:

- Letter formation

Nothing says summer quite like watermelons. This Quiet Bin is a *sweet* way to help little ones quietly practice letter formation.

Draw letters onto the pink paper plates and encourage little ones to trace those letters using the black watermelon seeds (buttons).

This Quiet Bin is great for helping little ones learn about letter formation and really play with the shapes of each letter.

It's a great idea to start with a child's name letters.

Dripping Popsicles

Materials:

- Popsicle sticks

- Construction Paper 'popsicles'

- Hole punched paper

Target skills:

- Fine motor skills

- Colour matching

Using many different colours of paper, cut small squares. Fold the squares in half and tape or glue the long side and one short side. Glue a popsicle stick to the open short side, leaving a gap. These are the popsicles.

Use the left over paper to hole punch lots of "drips." Or just cut tiny squares.

Little ones love accomplishing tasks and will work hard to put all of their drips back into the popsicles—and while they do they will be working on that pincer grip!

Making Sunshine

Materials:

- Yellow strips of paper

- Yellow circles

- Scissors

Target skills:

- Cutting

When children are learning to cut they will be content to spend loads of time practicing.

This Quiet Bin is perfect for toddlers and preschoolers who are practicing their scissor skills.

Simply prepare long skinny strips of yellow construction paper and yellow circles. Children can snip the yellow strips into small strips and place them around the yellow circles making the suns shine.

Adding numbers to the circles is a great way to add in some counting for older children.

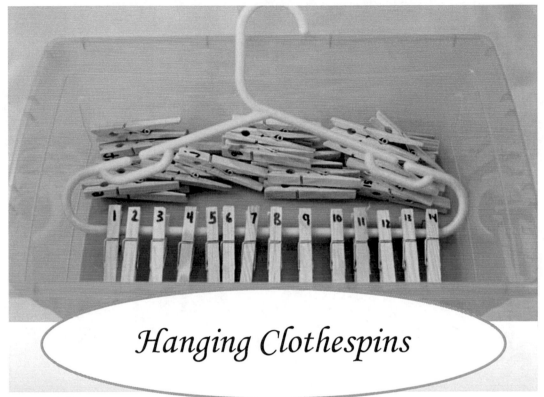

Hanging Clothespins

Materials:

- Hanger

- Clothespins with numbers

Target skills:

- Number recognition

- Number order

- Hand Strengthening

Clothespins mean summertime in our household. Clothes are hanging outside on our line every day in the summer. And often forgotten in the rain too. My record is towels that have hung outside for four straight days and nights drying and then getting rained on, again and again.

Clothespins are fantastic tools for children too. Pinching a clothespin is a great way to strengthen little hands for future writing.

Write numbers on the clothespins and children can practice recognizing and ordering numbers. Add in some shapes for children to practice patterning. Add in a marker and let them create their own games.

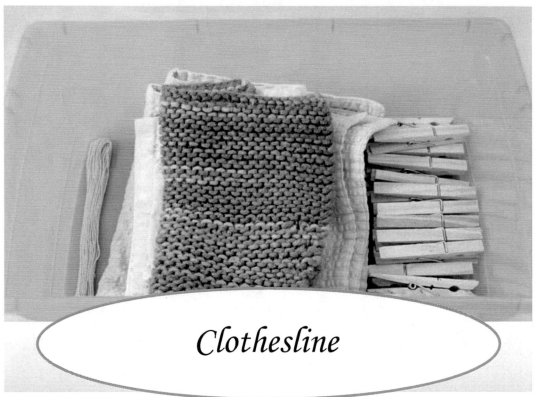

Clothesline

Materials:

- String

- Clothespins

- Doll clothes

Target skills:

- Imaginative play

- Strengthening hands

Children are master imitators. If you are one to hang clothes on your clothesline in the summer (or the rain) then your little ones are bound to love this Quiet Bin.

Tie the string between two chairs. Children can hang up doll clothing, socks, or bibs using the clothespins.

Imaginations will be given a good stretch with this one as little stories unfold throughout the play.

Add in a few unusual items to give little ones some interest in their storylines.

Popsicle Stick Colour Match

Materials:

- Popsicle sticks with ends painted

- Cards with shapes drawn on them

Target skills:

- Colour matching

- Creating shapes

Elaborate and beautiful designs and pictures will be created with this Quiet Bin.

Popsicle stick ends can be dipped in paint, or coloured with markers.

This makes the popsicle sticks very inviting to play and create with.

Little ones can be encouraged to match coloured ends together to see how long of a line can be made.

Older children can try to make different shapes. Shapes can be drawn on paper and added to the Quiet Bin for a bit of guidance.

Watermelon Lacing

Materials:

- Pink Paper Plates

- Green yarn

Target skills:

- Fine motor skills

- Hand-eye coordination

- Problem solving

Hole punch all around the edge of a pink paper plate. Next, cut some long green yarn or string.

Children can practice "wrapping" the green yarn around the outside of the paper plate as the rind.

For activities such as this one, I will often begin one watermelon and leave it in the Quiet Bin as inspiration ... though little ones may do it completely differently, which is perfectly fine.

Shells at the Beach

Materials:

- Brown play dough (or orange if you don't have brown!)
- Shells

Target skills:

- Imaginative play

I try to keep my Quiet Bins fairly mess free as I like my little ones to use them all on their own. This one does use playdough, but in our house it doesn't get very messy and is a favourite so I thought I would share.

Spread a layer of brown playdough over the bottom of the Quiet Bin and then add some seashells. You can use orange playdough if that is all you have and you need to take a picture for your book.

Little ones can explore making shapes and imprints by using the seashells as stamps. They can also experiment with the different textures of the shells.

The imaginative stories that come from a simple scene like this are fantastic.

Dry Erase Book

Materials:

- Summertime dot to dots, mazes, etc.

- Plastic page protectors

- Dry erase markers

Target skills:

- Dot to dot for number order and recognition

- Mazes for visual spatial skills and problem solving

This book is fantastic for a Quiet Bin anytime of the year really, just swap out the pages. It is also fabulous for road trips.

Print off some mazes and dot-to-dot pages from the computer. (I really like MrPrintables.com) This particular book we created had a summer focus with flowers, beach, sunshine, and swimming activities.

Pop them into clear plastic page protectors and put them into a binder, or just leave them loose in the Quiet Bin.

Little ones can complete the activities again and again using dry erase markers. Completing the same activity multiple times is actually a wonderful learning opportunity for children.

'Sandy' Letters

Materials:

- Squares of sandpaper

- Scraps of yarn

Target skills:

- Letter formation

Find some rough sandpaper and cut into squares. It doesn't need to be extremely rough, but the fine sand paper doesn't work well.

Write the letters of the alphabet in either upper or lowercase, one letter per sandpaper square. Word of warning, this will ruin your marker by the time you reach 'z'. Don't worry, it's worth it!

Next, cut some yarn and pop it into the Quiet Bin as well.

Little ones can practice letter formation again and again by tracing the letters in yarn.

Cheerios Birdfeeder

Materials:

- Cheerios

- Pipe cleaners

Target skills:

- Fine motor skills

- Nature learning

While this Quiet Bin might turn into a snack bin for many little ones, the snack is in fact meant for the birds.

Children can thread the cheerios onto the pipe cleaners and shape then into circles, twisting to secure.

These cute birdfeeders can be hung onto trees for feathery friends to enjoy.

Fall Quiet Bins

Whether your little ones are settling into life at school, settling into siblings being at school, or just settling into Fall, these Quiet Bins are lovely to calm.

Being at school all day can bring many a meltdowns when little ones return home. Often having a Quiet Bin and a snack ready when your child gets home can make all the difference.

Threading leaves onto trees, making silly monsters, or creating funny jack-o-lantern faces is a great way to spend Fall.

Googly Eye Monsters

Materials:

- Paper with Googly eyes glued on

- Crayons/markers

Target skills:

- Creativity

- Pencil grip

Monsters, babies, chickens, and pigs—this Quiet Bin certainly doesn't only produce monsters!

The open-endedness of this art exploration is perfect for children of all ages.

Adding two googly eyes to the piece of paper encourages little ones to create creatures with two eyes. Try adding a third to help little artists create unique three-eyed creatures, perfect for this holiday season.

Kleenex Ghosts

Materials:

- Kleenex

- Black marker

- Pipe cleaners

Target skills:

- Creativity

- Imaginative play

You know those ideas that are almost too simple? Those ideas that you wonder—will the kids even be into this? Well, I had thought that about this Quiet Bin, but let me assure you—huge hit!

Load up that Quiet Bin with tons of Kleenex, or just throw a whole box in. Add in pipe cleaners and a marker.

Children can ball up one Kleenex as a ghost head, wrap a flat Kleenex around, and secure around the neck with a pipe cleaner. Then they can draw on a spooky face and hang them all over the house.

Put the Fall Leaves on the Trees

Materials:

- Pipe cleaner trees

- Coloured buttons

Target skills:

- Colour sorting

- Fine motor skills

Twist 7 or 8 brown pipe cleaners together to create little bare trees. Add a few of these to this Quiet Bin with buttons the colour of fall leaves.

Little ones can thread the button Fall leaves on to the trees.

Trees can become patterned or sorted by colours.

Maybe little ones could put two buttons on each branch. Do they have enough to put 4 buttons on each branch? The possibilities for quiet play are infinite with this one.

Felt Jack-o-lantern

Materials:

- Felt pumpkins

- Black or yellow felt face pieces

Target skills:

- Imaginative Play

- Emotion learning

Learn all about emotions with this engaging Quiet Bin. Simply cut out orange pumpkin shapes from felt. Add in some black or yellow felt face pieces (eyes, nose, mouths).

Add in many different shapes for eyes and mouths to help your little one experiment with emotions.

Adding a mirror is a great way to extend this activity. Little ones can create the same emotions as their jack-o-lanterns.

Fall Leaf Rubbing

Materials:

- Real or fabric leaves
- Crayons
- Paper

Target skills:

- Learning about textures
- Nature learning

Creating leaf rubbings is a lovely, calming activity.

Add many different shapes of leaves to this Quiet Bin with many different colours of crayons. Encourage little ones to use the side of the crayon when doing their leaf rubbings for better results.

Try adding in Fall colours for the crayons: red, orange, and yellow.

Adding scissors will encourage little ones to cut our their leaf rubbings and practice cutting skills as well..

Spider Web Baskets

Materials:

- Plastic basket

- White yarn or string

- Spider rings

Target skills:

- Weaving

- Fine motor skills

Create a great big spider's web with this fun Quiet Bin. Little ones can weave in and out, back and forth, up and down, to create a tangled spider web.

Add in some black plastic spider rings, or tiny spiders cut out of black construction paper to add in some imaginative play.

Singing songs about spiders will encourage little ones to act out the songs. Try singing the itsy bitsy spider as your little one plays with this Quiet Bin.

Turkey Feathers

Materials:

- Styrofoam balls
- Coloured feathers
- Googly eyes

Target skills:

- Counting
- Fine motor skills
- Colour sorting

It wouldn't be Fall without a turkey Quiet Bin!

Add some googly eyes to Styrofoam balls and toss them into a Quiet Bin with oodles of coloured feathers. Don't worry if your spouse says they look like snowmen.

Little ones can decorate their turkeys by poking the feathers all over the Styrofoam balls.

Add math learning to this bin by adding numbers to the turkeys. Children can add that number of feathers to the balls. Or have little ones sort by colours.

Be sure to add in a tiny ball or two so turkey families come into play and little imaginations will take it from there.

Leaf Letter Matching

Materials:

- Paper tree shape

- Foam leaves

Target skills:

- Alphabet learning

- Letter matching

This Quiet Bin can be done in so many different ways for so many different skills.

A great activity is to draw a big tree with uppercase letters all over the branches. Older children can practice matching the leaves with lowercase letters drawn on them to the uppercase branches.

This could be done with numbers, shapes, even just squiggles to begin differentiating shapes.

It is helpful to have a sheet with the alphabet written in upper and lowercase in the bin so little ones can self-check their tree.

Squiggle Monsters

Materials:

- Blank paper with squiggles

- Markers

Target skills:

- Creativity

- Imaginative Play

This simple little activity is immensely engaging and calming. I use it all the time as a break activity when I am tutoring.

Simply take a piece of paper and add a squiggle—a line, a twist, a curly curl—anything.

Encourage little ones to turn this squiggle into Halloween creatures ... three eyed monsters, spooky pumpkins, jack-o-lanterns, or whatever they come up with.

Anytime Quiet Bins

It is a great idea to keep some Quiet Bins ready that can be used for anytime of the year.

These Quiet Bins are great for any season and can be used in lots of different locations too, like at restaurants, in the doctor's office, or while visiting Great Aunt Alice.

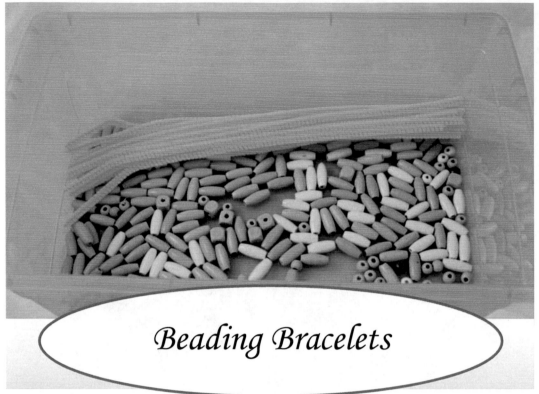

Beading Bracelets

Materials:

- Pipe cleaners

- Beads

Target skills:

- Fine motor skills

- Counting

- Colour sorting

This Quiet Bin is ALWAYS on hand in our house. It is used every single week by one of my little ones.

With lots of pipe cleaners and oodles of pretty beads, it just never gets old.

Sometimes we add in letter beads, wooden beads, or shaped beads just to spice things up. Most of the time, however, it is simply beads and pipe cleaners. And oodles of fun.

When finished these bracelets can be proudly given as gifts.

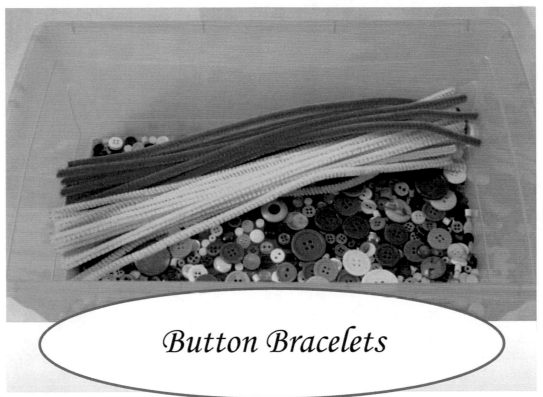

Button Bracelets

Materials:

- Pipe cleaners
- Buttons

Target skills:

- Fine motor skills
- Counting
- Colour sorting

This Quiet Bin is much like the beaded bracelets, but is geared towards slightly older children.

This Quiet Bin contains pipe cleaners or string and buttons. Children can thread up through one button hole and down through the other making the button lay flat.

Stacking buttons before threading them gives these bracelets lots of dimension and character.

Button bracelets also make charming gifts. Perhaps these could be added to the gift wrapping Winter Quiet Bin.

Cutting Bin

Materials:

- Scissors

- Things to snip: feathers, straws, paper, bands

Target skills:

- Cutting skills

- Learning about textures

One of the easiest bins to prepare, and a certain hit with any little ones, is one that encourages kids to learn how to use scissors.

Fill this Quiet Bin with little things perfect for snipping: feathers, construction paper strips, straws, rubber bands.

Be sure to vary the materials so little ones can experience cutting different textures. Cutting a rubber band is very different from cutting paper. Experiencing textures in many different ways is very valuable learning for little ones.

Sticker Trace a Name

Materials:

- File folder with names written

- Stickers

Target skills:

- Letter formation

- Letter and sight word recognition

This Quiet Bin could be done just with paper, but adding a file folder makes this activity extra special.

Write your child's name, family member names, letters of the alphabet, or sight words (all dependent on the stage your child is ready for) in a file folder.

Little ones can add stickers over top of the letters, tracing the letters with the stickers. This is a great activity to help little ones really focus on the shape and movement of each letter..

Sticky Foam Blocks

Materials:

- Foam Blocks

- Wet washcloth

Target skills:

- Building, stability

- Planning skills

Magic building! We found this whole package of foam blocks at our local dollar store.

At first, this was a Quiet Bin all in itself. But after a little while we discovered that adding in a wet cloth added in a magical dimension.

When little ones rub a wet cloth on the foam blocks they stick together much like glue.

With this neat addition, building can be taken to another level.

Basket Weaving

Materials:

- Plastic basket

- Pipe cleaners

Target skills:

- Fine motor skills

- Weaving

- Patterning

A favourite of my two year old's: basket weaving! Simply pop a basket with many holes and oodles of pipe cleaners in the Quiet Bin, and you are set.

Little ones can practice hand-eye coordination by poking the pipe cleaners in through the holes.

Older children can practice weaving their pipe cleaners in one hole and out the next.

Weaving is a wonderful way for children to develop patterning skills.

Bathmat Geo Board

Materials:

- Small, clean bathmat
- Elastics or rubber bands

Target skills:

- Fine motor skills
- Shapes

I had noticed the suction cups on the bottom of our bathmat and just knew there had to be a great Quiet Bin activity there somehow. And I found it!

We bought a new small bathmat, and added it to a quiet bin with some elastics. When the mat is stretched out on the ground, suction cup side up, it makes a fabulous geo board.

Elastics can be stretched around the suction cups making squares, triangles, and more complicated shapes too.

Older children will have fun making tricky pictures.

FURTHER READING

If you are interested in learning more about Waldorf, finding a rhythm to your day, or looking for suggestions on parenting books, I would highly recommend:

Baldwin Dancy, R. (2006). *You Are Your Child's First Teacher*. United Kingdom: Hawthorne Press.

Gurian, M. (1996). *The Wonder of Boys*. New York: Penguin Putnam.

Neufeld, Gordon. (2006). *Hold on to Your Kids: Why parents need to matter more than peers*. United States: Ballantine Books.

Williams, Lawrence. (2014). *The Heart of Learning*. Vermont: Oak Meadow.

ABOUT THE AUTHOR

Sarah Noftle is a Mama, Teacher, and Wanna-be Farmer (in that order). Having taught in the kindergarten classroom for many years, she opted to stay home with her own wild ones for awhile. Sarah now balances (sort of) being home with her children and working in the classroom part-time. She has a slight (not slight) chicken obsession, and shares her farm happily with 18 feathery ladies ... oh, and her husband and 3 children.

Visit her blog at: HowWeeLearn.com

Made in the USA
San Bernardino, CA
05 November 2016